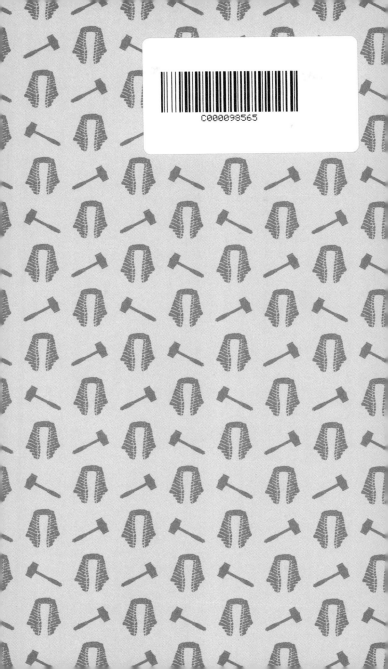

The Law
Is An

Richard Happer

With illustrations by
Joseph Hemmings

The Law Is An Ass
Published in the United Kingdom in 2012 by
Punk Publishing Ltd
3 The Yard
Pegasus Place
London
SE11 5SD

www.punkpublishing.co.uk

A catalogue record of this book is available from the British Library.

ISBN 978-1-906889-56-2

10 9 8 7 6 5 4 3 2 1

The Law
Is An

Richard Happer

With illustrations by
Joseph Hemmings

Contents

Introduction

How dare we ridicule The Law? What could be nobler than this dignified and age-old institution? What could be more worthy of respect than the intelligence and learning displayed by centuries of brilliant legal brains? What could be more valuable than this compendium of wisdom, drawn from precedent and common human morality, that punishes the wicked, protects the good and helps us live our everyday lives more harmoniously?

Well, The Law also says that it is illegal to have sex with a porcupine.

You see, it turns out that The Law makes its own pretty convincing case for being ridiculous. The obviously idiotic rulings. The rulings against the obviously idiotic. The endless interference with people's sex lives. Its bizarre hang-ups about nudity. The daft rules on eating and drinking. The cruel and vindictive punishments. The laughable attempts to legislate animals. And the outrageous results of what happens when lawyers try to win money for morons.

So, rather than lead the witness or tamper with the evidence, we here simply present real-life examples of statutes from around the world and ask you to make up your own mind.

In the case of The Law being an ass, will you find it guilty or not guilty?

Food and Drink Felonies

1. Having Your Cake and Eating It

Under UK law, VAT is not charged on chocolate-covered cakes, but is on chocolate-covered biscuits. This led to a problem when HM Customs and Excise claimed that Jaffa Cakes are biscuits and so should be taxed. Manufacturer McVities disagreed, defending Jaffa Cakes' status as cakes in court in 1991. McVities' lawyers ingeniously pointed out that biscuits go soft when stale, but cakes go hard. Since Jaffa Cakes do the latter, they must be a cake. The judge agreed, and VAT is not paid on Jaffa Cakes.

2. Guilty of Not Being a Crisp

The UK's 1994 VAT Act levied a 17.5 per cent tax on 'potato crisps, potato sticks, potato puffs and similar products made from the potato, or from potato flour, or from potato starch'. Proctor & Gamble, the makers of Pringles, used this ruling to save millions of pounds in VAT. They went to the High Court to have their product legally ruled as not being a crisp, pointing out that only 42 per cent of a Pringle is potato. (Not something you'd think they'd want to admit in court, but there you go.)

3. Unap'peel'ing Onions

Barbers in Waterloo, Nebraska, are forbidden from eating onions between 7am and 7pm, on penalty of a fine and having their shop closed. In Oregon, it is ministers about to deliver a sermon who can't eat garlic or onions. Any West Virginia kids who have a test they want to avoid should simply do a spot of woodland grazing on the way to school in the morning – local law states that you may not attend class with your breath smelling of 'wild onions'.

4. Free Fruit Fiasco

The US Tariff Act of 1872 laid down the law when it came to what could be imported tax-free: 'fruit plants, tropical and semi-tropical, for the purpose of propagation'. But a bungling legal clerk had misplaced a comma; the line should have read 'fruit, plants tropical and semi-tropical'. Unfortunately for the Government, fruit importers had their eyes peeled and state coffers were soon down a juicy $1 million.

5. You're Nut Making a Whole Lot of Sense

The way some laws are worded opens up multiple interpretations. This one, however, is unique in not having any possible interpretation at all. A judge of the Court of Session in Scotland once made the following decisive ruling: 'In the Nuts (unground), (other than groundnuts) Order, the expression "nuts" shall have reference to such nuts, other than groundnuts, as would but for this amending Order not qualify as nuts (unground) (other than groundnuts) by reason of their being nuts (unground)'.

6. A Legal Slip-Up

If you're going to drop fruit peel in Woodstock, Oxfordshire, make sure it's a banana skin. An ancient local statute is very clear that it is illegal to drop fruit peel on the streets of the town. However, the law very specifically mentions only citrus fruits, not bananas. Which is kind of bananas, really.

7. Legally Legless

Why did they invent bourbon in Kentucky? Is it because the area is perfect for growing maize? Because the water is pure? Because lots of Scots–Irish immigrants with knowledge of distilling settled there? Well, possibly. Or maybe it's because state law stipulates that a person is considered sober until he or she 'cannot hold onto the ground'.

8. I Arresht You in the Name of the... Hic!

You might think that a pub is a good place for getting drunk. But according to the UK Licensing Act 1872 – which still applies – it is actually illegal to be drunk in a pub or bar. The Criminal Justice and Police Act 2001 went one step further and empowered police officers to impose fines for drunkenness. They can't then spend the money on booze themselves – it's illegal to serve a constable on duty. But the 1872 Act thoughtfully allows them to drink in licensed premises after closing time.

9. Royal Rum Regatta

Every Royal Navy ship entering the Port of London must give a barrel of rum to the Constable of the Tower of London. You'd think that would mean he'd be swimming in booze but, actually, very few Royal Navy ships enter the city these days. The tradition is maintained annually, however, when a vessel moors at Tower Pier and the captain and several of his men hand a barrel over. The Constable, the Yeoman Warders and the sailors then go and drink it. Presumably because none of them have anything better to do, like protecting the Crown Jewels or our nation, for example.

10. I Arrest Chew in the Name of the Law

Ever thought that chewing gum could land you in jail? Well, in Singapore, it has been completely illegal since 1992. The only exception is nicotine gum, but even then smokers can only get it from a pharmacy with a prescription. Chewing gum is legal in New York, of course, but cinema owners there must chisel all gum off the undersides of their auditorium seats every month. Makes trodden-in popcorn seem positively pleasant.

11. And What Do You Do?

The City of London Coroner is obviously an important and necessary person, as is the Commissioner of Sewers. But the 'Garbler'? A person who, in the 16th century, removed the impurities in spices by sifting them? Well, according to clause 14 of the City of London Elections Act 1724, an official Garbler is one of the positions that the city can still appoint rather than go to the trouble of electing. Maybe they should sift out a duff law or two instead.

12. Drunken Disorders

Drinking a lot is confusing enough without having to remember a myriad of boozing bylaws. For example, in St Louis you can't drink beer while sitting on a city street, but in Chicago you can be arrested for drinking standing up anywhere in the city. You cannot be served wine in a teacup in Topeka, Kansas; while in Cleveland, no more than one person may sip from a whisky bottle. Saskatchewan in Canada at least has the rights of the drinker at its civic heart – it is against the law to drink water in beer parlours there.

13. Would Sir Like Some Steak With His Steak?

Back in the glory days of Sparta, if you were male you legally had to consume two pounds of meat a day. You were also forbidden from drinking too much, and had to be married before you turned 30. You were probably gagging for it by that point, so it would have made no difference that your bride was required by law to have her head shaved on your wedding night.

14. Where's that Dessert Trolley?

When dining at a restaurant in Denmark, you don't have to pay for your food unless, by your own opinion, you are 'full' at the end of your meal. A wafer-thin mint, sir?

15. Latte of the Night

Coffee-shop owners are expressly forbidden from serving known prostitutes. Likewise, juice-bar owners would be in big trouble if they got caught selling a smoothie to a reputed thief. In fact, any establishment that sells refreshments is forbidden from serving any type of 'disorderly person' whatsoever. Makes you wonder why they have a bar in the Houses of Parliament…

16. Candyland

In Idaho, boxes of candy given as romantic gifts must weigh more than 50 pounds. Meanwhile one town in the state, Pocatello, has decreed that it's 'prohibited for pedestrians and motorists to display frowns, grimaces, scowls, threatening and glowering looks, gloomy and depressed facial appearances, generally all of which reflect unfavourably upon the city's reputation'. Presumably that's not a problem given the amount of sweets everyone's eating.

17. The Food Is Rubbish Here

It sure is hard being a down-and-out in Texas. Homeless and starving, your dignity in tatters, you rake around in a bin for scraps to eat rather than stealing food. Whereupon the bin's owner calls the cops and has you arrested, charged and thrown in jail – he's within his rights to do so. Talk about kicking a man when he's down. Ah well, at least in prison the food is free.

18. In a Bit of a Pickle

The law can bite down hard when it comes to eating and drinking. In Turkey, in the 16th and 17th centuries, you could be put to death for drinking coffee. In Cambodia, the law was harsh on people who bullied helpless edible plants – you faced a fine for 'insulting rice'. In New Jersey you still must not eat pickles on Sundays and, if you bite into a bad one on any other day, don't whatever you do throw it in the street – the cops will can you.

19. Do Ya Feel Hungry, Punk?

Legislators in the town of Carmel, California, were some of the most evil sons of bitches ever to walk the earth – they had outlawed ice-cream parlours in the town. Then the good citizens elected Clint Eastwood as their Mayor, and he blew that dumbass law right off the statute books.

20. A Full Slice of Pie

If you find yourself in a restaurant in Memphis, Tennessee, you must remember not to give any of your pie to fellow diners, no matter how much they plead. It is also illegal to take unfinished pie home. All pie must be eaten on the premises. For a while it was thought this law was to prevent Elvis feeling bad for his gargantuan appetite. However, since the same state has gone to the trouble of making it illegal to use a lasso to catch a fish, it could be down to a more fundamental problem with the justice system.

21. Fat Fighters

You are forbidden to be fat in Japan. Although their country already has one of the world's lowest obesity rates (less than 5 per cent, in contrast to the USA's 35 per cent), that didn't stop Japanese lawmakers from setting a maximum waistline size in 2009. Every man aged 40 and over must not have a waist measuring 80cm or above, every woman, 90cm or above. And this from the land that brought us sumo wrestling…

22. Yellow Peril

Margarine is naturally greyish–white in colour, and Canadian manufacturers were, for a long time, banned from adding dyes that made it butter-coloured. It had to appear in tubs in its less-than-appealing natural state. Quebec only repealed this law in 2008. Could dairy farmers have had something to do with introducing this piece of legislation?

23. Bonkers Beer Bylaws

In North Dakota, no bar can serve beer and pretzels at the same time. That might sound crazy, but in Texas it is illegal to take more than three sips of beer at a time, while standing. And that same state has banned the entire Encyclopaedia Britannica because it explains how to make beer at home. In Nebraska, it is illegal for bar owners to sell beer unless they are simultaneously brewing a kettle of soup. Simple solution: just make it beer soup.

24. The Indelicate Delicacy

The people of Brunei, Indonesia and Malaysia simply love the durian fruit, which looks a little like a cross between a pineapple and a porcupine. However, many local authorities have completely banned the consumption of this delicacy from buses, subways, hotels and airports. Is this yet another outrageous infringement of civil liberties? Well, since the durian is said to smell like a mixture of 'pig-shit, turpentine and onions', maybe not, on this occasion.

25. Pi in the Sky

In 1897, the Indiana General Assembly passed Bill #246, which stated that the mathematical constant of π (the ratio of a circle's circumference to its diameter) was not 3.14159265... as had previously been suspected, but 3.2. This made things so much neater from a legal point of view. It should, in fairness, be pointed out that the Bill was initially debated by the Committee on Swamp Lands. Their error, however, is nothing compared with the Second Book of Chronicles in the Bible, which implies that π has the value of 3.

Love, Lust and The Law

26. Crimes of Passion

In Florida, any form of sexual contact other than the 'missionary' position is deemed a misdemeanour. Think it doesn't matter because the couples are in the privacy of their own home when they're getting steamy? Wrong. There have been cases – even recently – of police entering premises, with a warrant for another charge, and catching the home's residents violating this law. And, in those cases, the offending felons were arrested and charged.

27. Paying Lip-Service to The Law

In Indiana, anyone with a moustache who 'habitually kisses human beings' could be in big trouble. And you must not kiss for more than one second in Halethorpe, Maryland, no matter how smooth the upper lips of the parties concerned. These laws might sound frivolous but, in the 18th century, a Boston sailor who had been at sea for three years had the nerve to kiss his wife in public on his return, on a Sunday. The prudish judiciary locked him in the stocks for two hours. It would hardly have been surprising if, when they let him out, he just got straight back on his boat.

28. Girl Power

The UK's Criminal Law Amendment Act 1885 was particularly tough on 'gross indecency' between men – it was this law that caught Oscar Wilde with his pants down. But it makes no mention of lesbian activities, reputedly because Queen Victoria insisted that 'women don't do such things'. All references to lesbianism were removed from the Act to avoid offending her majesty, making it perfectly legal.

29. Sin(free) City

A weekend of low-down fun in a high-class hotel is one of life's most naughty pleasures. But do remember that in London it is illegal to register under an assumed name for your nookie. 'Falsifying a hotel registration' for sex can cost you a fine of £20 and you'll be shown the door. All of which puts the love-struck couple in a tight spot, because making out in buses, trains, parked cars, churches and parks is also forbidden.

30. Just Popping Out for Lunch

For anyone in need of letting off steam during the working day, move to New Mexico and find a job there. The reason? It's legal for couples to have sex in a parked vehicle during their lunch break from work, so long as the car/van/campervan has its curtains drawn to stop strangers from stealing a glance inside. Not such good news for those who favour two-wheeled means of transport, though.

31. As Mum is My Witness

If you think that going out for a meal with your mother-in-law is bad, just be thankful you don't live in Cali, Colombia. The law in this part of the world states that women can only have sex with their husband (fair enough) and that the first time they do, their mothers have to 'witness the act'. (Um…)
Is she meant to offer tips? Encouragement? And who is prosecuted if she misses the event? Frankly, that's enough of that one.

32. He Lost His Head

You might think that if anything is one person's private business it's masturbation. But no, the law gets its mitts on that too. Oklahoma Senator Constance Johnson has added a clause to Senate Bill 1433, which would make 'any action in which a man ejaculates or otherwise deposits semen anywhere but in a woman's vagina' illegal. Meanwhile in Indonesia, the ultimate penalty for masturbation was once said to be decapitation.

33. Doggy Style

There's nothing like a dog jumping on your bed to put you off your love-making activities. But if you're on the job in Bristol, UK, it's against the law to push your pooch off the bed. Rover is quite within his rights to watch. It is, however, perfectly acceptable to kick your cat out. And neither animal should even think of joining in, of course, as that would be against the Sexual Offences Act 1956.

34. Kiss Me Quick

Who said romance is dead? In Iowa, kisses may last for as many as, but no more than, five whole minutes. So, if you're in the mood for a good long snog, be sure to set that stopwatch before puckering up. On the bright side, at least there's no chance Iowans will make a challenge for the Guinness Book of World Records' 'longest kiss' marathon.

35. Paws for Thought

Should your animals be feeling amorous towards each other, you had better not be in Scotland's Montrose. There, a bylaw specifically forbids pets and even livestock from mating within the town boundaries. Their owner faces 25 days in jail and a £15 fine for any such farmyard friskiness. Not a great town for dog breeders, then.

36. Carnal Knowledge

You have to be careful about getting passionate in your car in Bedfordshire's Leighton Buzzard, where drivers are not allowed to kiss a passenger while tootling along 'winding roads'. Although snogging on straight roads is presumably okay. In Edinburgh, you can make love on your back seat, but only if you are parked in your own driveway. While in Bristol, however, you can bonk away anywhere inside the car, but under no circumstances should you make love underneath your vehicle.

37. Fling Sting

Until 1973, a cuckolded husband in England could claim damages from his wife's lover. The fornicators were said to have indulged in 'criminal conversation'. A wronged wife could also sue, but if the 'other woman' was also married it was her husband who had to shell out. Paying for your wife's adultery does seem particularly harsh. But it's nothing on what male adulterers could expect in the 12th century – castration followed by blinding.

38. Stairway to Heaven

Birmingham boasts Britain's sexiest churches. A local bylaw maintains that no couple may have sex 'on the steps of any church after the sun goes down'. This was obviously a bit of a problem locally, and offenders risk the weighty charge of disorderly conduct and a fine of £25 each. Strangely, however, the statute says nothing about church-step romps while the sun is up…

Parliamentary Privileges

39. A Result You Can Bank On

'**O**ne man, one vote' is a sacred principle of British democracy – unless you live in the City of London, that is. There, companies are legally allowed to vote in local elections. And the companies get more votes the bigger they are – the largest employer can cast 79 votes. With only 9,000 actual residents in the borough, and thousands more companies, is it any wonder that the banks seem to be able to do exactly what they want?

40. Big Benefits

Security in England's Parliament is understandably strict but, legally, the Palace of Westminster is a public building, which you are free to enter, within some limits. Better still, every constituent has the legal right to ask his or her MP for a free tour of the clock tower. If you can bear the din, it's even possible to stand next to the iconic Big Ben bell as it strikes the hours.

41. Inflammatory Boots, Not Books

England's Parliament is still allowed to burn books, which it frequently used to do when it believed the publications were seditious. The public hangman usually did the burning in Palace Yard. When he tried to ignite copies of an anti-royal article by John Wilkes in 1763, the crowd lobbed stones at him until he stopped and, rather randomly, burned a petticoat and a pair of boots instead. There haven't been any governmental book-burnings since.

42. Cooking the Books

Interestingly, while Parliament can carbonise copies of whatever it likes, mere citizens are forbidden by the Malicious Damage Act 1861 from doing the same. Playwright Joe Orton and his lover Kenneth Halliwell got six months in prison for burning books in 1962. The act forbids the damage or destruction of anything kept 'for the purpose of art, science or literature'. Which, presumably, means they couldn't nab us for lobbing Hansard on a bonfire.

43. Day and Knight

I t is illegal to enter the Houses of Parliament in a suit of armour. This law even has its own Act, rather descriptively entitled 'A Statute forbidding Bearing of Armour', dated 1313. This is ironic, if you think about it: how many of the distinguished fellows who sit on those famous green leather benches have, in fact, been knighted and so, back in the day, would themselves have worn armour? King Arthur and his Round Table compadres would be aghast.

44. Rocket Regulation

As Guy Fawkes found out to his cost, blowing up the Houses of Parliament is really not acceptable. But, technically, it's also illegal to celebrate his demise in the traditional way. Section 28 of the Town Police Clauses Act 1847 promises a £1,000 fine for 'every person who wantonly discharges any firearm, or throws or discharges any stone or other missile, or makes any bonfire, or throws or sets fire to any firework'.

45. Will the Honourable Gentleman Please Come to Heel?

It's a mystery why there are so many empty seats in Parliament, especially as, thanks to a venerable law dating from 1382, members of both the Houses of Lords and Commons must come 'when called'. If the MP doesn't have a decent excuse (buying a duck house does not count), he or she can be fined. Perhaps the speaker needs a louder whistle. Or a nice tennis ball they could all chase after.

46. Badge of Dishonour

Britain's Public Order Act 1936 was brought in to curb the antics of Oswald Mosley's fascists; it criminalised '… any person who in any public place or at any public meeting wears uniform signifying his association with any political organisation or with the promotion of any political object'. Which means it is actually a crime to wear a rosette for a political party in public. Who's up for going onstage at the next Tory party conference and making a citizen's arrest of David Cameron?

Criminal Creatures

47. Horse and Effect

Calgary takes its equestrian legislation extremely seriously. All businesses in the Canadian city are required to have a hitching post outside their establishment. Even if you get into a barney with a bar owner because there isn't one, and your horse wanders off, there's no need to worry; if you're kicked out of Calgary, you are entitled to a horse and a day's worth of rations to see you safely to the next city.

48. Terpsichorean Terrapin

If you're ever in Malaysia and the rhythm takes you, just make sure your dancing partner isn't a turtle. The law there forbids people from dancing on their backs. Key West in Florida hasn't ruled against dancing on turtles, but the statute is very clear about not racing them within the city limits... Or there'll be shell to pay.

49. Not Let Off the Hook

Worms aren't exactly a protected species, but there are many places where you aren't allowed to dig for them. A fisherman on the River Blackwater, near Maldon in Essex, found this out to his cost when a water bailiff cited a law dating back to 1171 and arrested him for unearthing some bait. He was fined £50. The bailiff said it was because the man's boat was damaging an oyster bed, but really it was because bailiffs just love to watch you squirm.

50. Dumbo Rules

You have to be very careful what you do with your wild animals in America. In North Carolina, for example, it is illegal to use elephants to plough cotton fields. And in Florida, if you tie your elephant to a parking meter, you must pay the same fee as you would for a vehicle. Should you find yourself in Baltimore, you are forbidden from taking your lion to the movies but, crucially, that statute says nothing about elephants, so why not just pick up a Jumbo popcorn and relax.

51. Lord of the Jungle

When Lord Byron was at Cambridge University, there was a rule forbidding students to keep dogs in their rooms. The infamously 'mad, bad and dangerous to know' poet followed that regulation to the letter. And kept a bear instead. The dons could do nothing.

52. Down the Swanny

Geese and ducks may be fair game, but if you're thinking of roasting a swan this Sunday, think again. Swans were declared the property of the British Crown in the 12th century. If you got caught pinching one you could expect a trip to the Tower of London. Today you will still be prosecuted – a man was jailed for two months in 2006 for killing and eating a swan from a boating pond in Llandudno.

53. That Kodiak Moment

In Alaska it is perfectly legal to shoot bears – but only with a gun. If you want to shoot one with a camera, you have to be very careful as far as the law is concerned as waking a sleeping bear for the purpose of taking a photograph is prohibited. Waking a sleeping bear to shoot him is not illegal, just very, very dumb. Presumably the safest and most law-abiding tactic is to pop a cap up his furry ass while he's hibernating – and then take his picture.

54. Beware of the Sleepy Old Fleabag

Be careful about displaying a 'beware of the dog' sign to deter burglars. In the UK, a bitten burglar could argue in court that such a sign shows you knew your dog was dangerous and so are liable for damages. If you display no sign then the court would decree that you were unaware of the threat of the animal, so are not liable. However, if your dog is a softy, a sign could still act as a deterrent. As long as you aren't honest, of course.

55. Raven Mad

A law introduced by Charles II states that six ravens must reside in the Tower of London at all times. Now, corvids may be among the brightest of birds, but they aren't known for their ability to read legal statutes. That's probably why the Yeoman Warder Ravenmaster at the Tower clips their wings. Good job too – if the ravens ever leave the Tower, legend has it that the building, and indeed the kingdom, will fall. Makes you wonder why Charles went to the trouble of drafting such a hugely risky decree in the first place.

56. Moose Misrule

Moose are troublemakers. That's the only explanation for the slew of moose-related legislation in Alaska. In Fairbanks it is forbidden to give beer or wine or any other alcoholic beverage to a moose. Nor are moose allowed on the pavement, even if sober. And you are not allowed to look at a moose from an aeroplane, even if you've spotted one dancing gleefully on the pavement smashed out of its hairy moose skull.

57. Fishy Tales

If your goldfish likes to travel, please think twice before you take him or her to the United States. In Seattle, goldfish are only permitted to ride the city buses in bowls if they keep still. So, if you can teach your scaly pet to play dead, then you'll both stay on the right side of the law and can happily board a bus there. Otherwise, it's best to leave Goldie (and the bowl) at home.

58. Udderly Ridiculous

It's a curious quirk of the law in Scotland that if a cow wanders through a gap in a hedge and onto his neighbour's land, then scoffs a few cauliflowers, the farmer-owner is liable for damages to his neighbour. However, if the cow wanders through the gap onto a road and causes a bus to crash with tragic and fatal consequences, the farmer is under no liability at all. Even if the cow in question was looking for cauliflowers at the time.

59. What Daisy Did Next

The previous law was proven in Inverness in 1954, when a cow escaped from a cattle auction onto the street, made its way into a building, up a staircase and into a room. It then promptly fell through the floorboards into the shop below, where it somehow turned on a tap that caused a flood. The shopkeeper sued the auctioneers, but the judge said that a 'gate-crashing, stair-climbing, floor-bursting, tap-turning cow' was something for which 'the law affords no remedy unless there was foreknowledge of some such propensities'. Obviously.

60. Antisocial Animals

Dumb animals? Don't you believe it – they're hiding something, and the law can prove it. Like in Switzerland, in 1471, when a cockerel was found guilty of laying an egg 'in defiance of natural law' and was executed. Or in Seville, in 1983, when a German Shepherd was arrested for stealing women's handbags. And officials in Stelvio, Italy, issued an arrest warrant in 1519 for a gang of moles that had damaged crops. The moles never showed up in court, so they must have been guilty.

61. Pass Me My Larger Oxen-Net, Will You?

The Constable of the Tower of London owns all the vegetation growing on Tower Hill. This may sound good but, in reality, this only amounts to grass (and any mouldy bits of fruit lying by the underground station). However, he is also entitled to first dibs on any carts that fall into the Tower moat and any horses, oxen, pigs or sheep that fall off London Bridge. Owners who want their animal back have to pay a penny a foot. Tourists don't count.

62. You Sound a Little Hoarse

The Cambridgeshire town of Newmarket once forbade people from 'going about the street with head cold or distemper' and from blowing their noses in public. This might seem like a very forward piece of public health legislature but, actually, it was designed to protect the delicate health of the hundreds of thoroughbred racehorses that are trained there.

63. Criminal Critters

No creature is above the law. Not even animals in the US. In Illinois, critters can be sent to jail just the same as humans. In Chicago, a monkey was found guilty of shoplifting and had to pay the penalty: five days in jail. A similar spate of monkey business in South Bend, Indiana, saw a primate convicted for smoking a cigarette (a crime thereabouts) and sentenced to pay a fine of $25, plus the cost of the trial. (Sources are unclear as to how these costs were paid by said monkey.)

64. But My Gorilla Gets Scared in the Front...

In Massachusetts, no gorilla is allowed in the back seat of any car. In Montana, it is sheep that are banned from the cab of your truck – unless you have a chaperone. And lawmakers in Minnesota don't mind too much about mammals, but they do insist that you can't cross state lines with a duck on top of your head; if you want to keep the sun out of your eyes, just wear a hat like everyone else.

65. ... And My Donkey is Dirty

Always check local laws when looking after animals: you may be contravening some very particular statutes. In Georgia, for example, donkeys must not be kept in bathtubs. And it is completely illegal to tie an alligator to a fire hydrant in Louisiana – it's so inconvenient for the fire brigade.

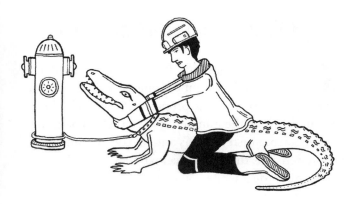

66. Dictators Just Have No Sense of Humour

In France, it has long been illegal to call or address a pig as 'Napoleon'. You might think this law would no longer be in force, but in the French translation of George Orwell's *Animal Farm*, the pig of that name was called 'César'. Mind you, Orwell based the character on Stalin, who probably wouldn't have been amused at the pig reference either.

67. Barking Mad Bylaws

In Oklahoma, dogs must have a permit signed by the mayor if they want to congregate in groups of three or more on private property. Presumably this is to cut down on the number of kitsch artists painting them playing poker. Ohio's animal laws are much more sensible: there, a policeman may bite a dog to quiet him. Meanwhile if you lose your pet tiger in the state, you must notify the authorities within one hour. It's only polite.

68. No Horsing Around

Equine lovers watch out – in Fountain Inn, South Carolina, all horses must wear pants. And in Wilbur, Washington, you can't ride an ugly horse. In parts of Iowa, your horse is forbidden from eating fire hydrants. While, should you and your steed fall foul of the law in Prescott, Arizona, you can ride him/her into the lobby of the county courthouse, but just don't even think about taking him up the stairs…

Know Your Place

69. Beheading for Branding Bedding?

Linen manufacturer Denis Pamphilon decided to celebrate Scotland's heroic (ahem) 1978 FIFA World Cup campaign by producing souvenir bedspreads featuring the country's heraldic red lion rampant. But, thanks to a law of 1672 that had never been repealed, he was dragged, terrified, before the Lyon Court – Scotland's Court of Chivalry – and charged with 'usurpation', the ultimate penalty for which was death by decapitation. Sensing that cutting off a businessman's head for making quilts was a bit of an overreaction, the Lyon Court eventually fined him £100 a day for as long as he made the bedspreads.

70. Catch-22 Customs

If you ever suffer at the rubber-gloved hands of a suspicious and painfully overzealous British customs officer, don't be tempted to take him or her to court – no matter how innocent you are. Section 268 of the Customs Laws Consolidation Act 1876 rules that no action can be brought against such an official without one month's notice. While Section 272 of the same Act insists that any action must be started within one month of the incident.

71. Lording It

Until 1948, peers had the right to be tried for their misdemeanours in the House of Lords, rather than an ordinary court. This made it possible for a woman to be married to two men but not be guilty of bigamy as long as she was first married to a commoner and then to a noble. As a peeress she would be tried in the House of Lords, but that would mean recognising her first marriage and negating her peerage and the House's own jurisdiction – so she would have to be acquitted. Even if a crown court nicked her, it would have to acknowledge her peerage and so also disqualify its right to try her. Again, she would walk free.

72. Some Are More Equal Than Brothers

After a coup d'état in Yemen, the head of the new regime issued the following decree: 'All official titles used in correspondence, addresses, mass media and in various official quarters will be completely abolished, to be replaced by the word "brother" at all levels'. It was signed by one 'Lieutenant Colonel Ibrahim al-Hamdi, President of the Military Command Council and Commander-in-Chief of the Armed Forces'.

73. The Unfair Fare

The law has often been less than even in its treatment of the social classes. In the 17th century, a ferryman and a passenger were arguing about the boat's fare when the passenger had the temerity to call the swan on the ferryman's badge a 'goose'. The ferryman referred this to the snooty Earl Marshal's Court, which decided that, as the swan emblem was that of an earl, the passenger had ridiculed the nobility and must pay a fine for this 'dishonour'. The fine was so enormous that it financially ruined the passenger.

74. Nose-Job, Medieval-Style

In feudal England, the law was what your lord said it was, meaning serfs often got a rough deal. It wasn't uncommon for a servant to have his nose slit, ears sliced off or to lose a hand – all for the heinous crime of spilling wine. And the ancient right of sanctuary, by which robbers, rapists and murderers could claim asylum in a church, did not apply to servants. They were simply hauled away from the altar by force.

75. Rent Rebate

You may find this shocking, but aristocratic favouritism continues to this day. The Duke of Marlborough rents his Oxfordshire estate, complete with 187-room Blenheim Palace (one of the largest houses in England) and its 2,100-acre park, from the Crown. The law decrees that the only payment he must make in return is to present the Blenheim Standard to the sovereign every year in August. Not that the Duke waves this flag of course; a servant does that for him.

76. Passport Piss-Take

You're a British citizen, you pay upwards of £77.50 for your passport, it has a valid picture of you in it – so it's yours, right? Well, maybe. According to the text on the flyleaf it belongs to Her Majesty's Government. But in 1955, Earl Jowitt, a former solicitor-general and attorney-general, pointed out that 'the Government' couldn't own anything because there is no such legal entity. No one since has been able to clarify the matter. So who the hell has the £77.50?

Sentenced to Transportation

77. Big Apple Bunny-Blasting Ban

If it's true that New York is a much safer place nowadays than it was in the past, it must in part be thanks to the law that forbids citizens from 'shooting at a rabbit from a moving trolley bus'. California takes traveller safety one step further – there it is a misdemeanour to shoot at any kind of game at all from any moving vehicle. Unless, of course, you are shooting at whales. Those blubbery buffoons deserve everything they get.

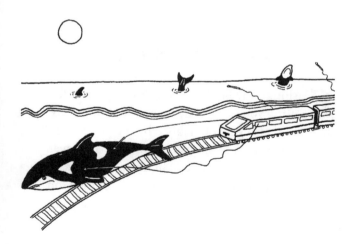

78. I Am Legally Entitled to a Cheese Sandwich

As air travel became increasingly popular in the early 20th century, many countries passed stringent safety laws. The state of Delaware went one further, putting passenger comfort on the statute books as well. In 1929 it ruled that persons in aircraft 'flying over large bodies of water shall be provided with an adequate supply of food and potable water'. Interestingly, it says nothing about duty-free perfume or scratch cards.

79. Flashing Fiasco

Flashing LED lights on your bike are great for getting you noticed by drivers, but in the UK they could also get you nabbed by the police. Until 2005 they weren't technically legal at all and, even now, they must flash at 60–240 times a minute. Even more curiously, they shouldn't be too bright. God forbid that truck drivers should actually see you.

80. Baaad Driving

It is unlawful, as well as slightly unhygienic, to drive with a sheep in your car in the UK. In 2000, police in England were surprised to see a fluffy ewe happily taking the air out of the open back window of a passing car. The driver protested that it was a family pet being driven to the woods for a walk. There was no prosecution, but a warning was issued. He got a second warning for the unsecured dog in the front seat. Yes, it was a sheepdog.

81. Plague Carriers

Flagging down a moving taxi is actually against the law in the UK; you really ought to go to a rank or other 'place appointed'. And, before you get in, the driver should ask if you are afflicted with any 'notifiable disease such as smallpox or the plague'. Alas, this isn't out of concern for your welfare but for the cabbie's own pocket – he can be fined for transporting a corpse.

82. Czech Your Change

If you're in Prague and your taxi driver ups the meter setting beyond the standard rate of 'level 1', watch out. If he turns it to 'level 2' he might just be ripping you off – par for the tourist course. But if he cranks it all the way to 'level 3' then it's time to panic. This is the official Government-sanctioned rate that must be used for all taxi rides following a nuclear explosion.

83. Taken for a Ride

According to the UK Licensing Act of 1872, being drunk in charge of a horse incurs a £200 fine and up to 51 weeks in jail. The same is true if you are squiffy while looking after a cow. Or a steam engine. This is probably fair enough – you don't want any of those things careering about the place if you nod off. But this worthwhile law neglects to say anything about being in charge of a drunken horse, which is surely far more dangerous.

84. Burn, Baby, Burn

If you're going to be caught in a fire, make sure you aren't in New Britain, Connecticut. Fire engines must obey the town's 25 mph speed limit, even when responding to an emergency. New Orleans is also pretty dangerous – fire engines must stop at all red lights. And you should avoid Fort Madison, Iowa, completely: its firemen are required to practise for 15 minutes before attending any fire.

85. Preparation is Everything

If you're touring in Switzerland by car and wear glasses, you must pack an extra pair in your glove box. And should you find yourself tooting through Pleasantville, Iowa, of an evening, make sure you've packed a man with a red lantern – you'll need him to walk in front of your car.

86. Rocketing Along

But that's nothing to Pennsylvania, where 'Any motorist driving along a country road at night must stop every mile and send up a rocket signal, wait 10 minutes for the road to be cleared of livestock, and then continue… Any motorist who sights a team of horses coming towards him must pull well off the road, cover his car with a blanket or canvas that blends with the countryside and let the horses pass. If the horses appear skittish, the motorist must take his car apart – piece by piece – and hide it under the nearest bushes'. If the horses weren't skittish before all those shenanigans, they sure will be afterwards.

87. Blind Drink-Driving

In London, you must be sitting in the front seat while driving. Memphis drivers are specifically required by law to be awake while driving. Birmingham, Alabama, maintains that you must not be blindfolded while driving. This sort of regulation might seem unnecessary, but police in Mississippi stopped a car that was zigzagging all over the road and found the driver was blind. It turned out that he was being directed by a chum in the passenger seat, who explained that he was too drunk to drive himself.

88. Continental Cruising

In Athens, Greece, they have some pretty strict motoring codes: you may not drive your car on public roads if you are 'poorly dressed' or 'un-bathed'. But in Bologna, Italy, they are much more relaxed. A law uniquely applying to prostitutes states that such persons may, 'drive a car carefully and at the same time lead a scandalous life'. And if the behaviour of Italy's former Prime Minister is anything to go by, yes, they probably mean at exactly the same time.

89. Bearly Legal

On the other hand, some cities have extremely sensible motoring legislation. Take Tacoma, Washington where 'it is mandatory for a motorist with criminal intentions to stop at the city limits and telephone the Chief of Police as he is entering town'. You aren't allowed to carry dogs in ambulances in Westport, Massachusetts; while in Missouri, you are strictly forbidden to let an uncaged bear ride in your boot or the front seat. He could play havoc with your shopping.

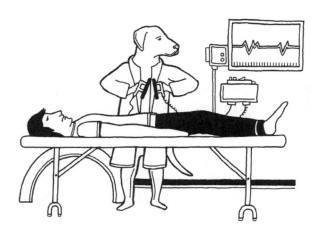

90. One for the Road

You might think that 'one for the road' is a phrase from the dark days of limited drink-driving legislation. But it actually originates from public hangings in London. The condemned prisoner would leave Newgate Prison on a route to Tyburn Gallows along what is now Oxford Street, and each publican would offer him a free drink: 'one for the road'. This was as much to get drinkers into his own hostelry as it was for charity – the processions were raucous events that drew massive crowds, took hours and brought traffic grinding to a halt. Sounds much like Oxford Street today, really.

91. He's a Total Cyclepath

If you're a UK resident, next time you're in a bad mood after a bust-up with your dearly beloved, whatever you do, don't get on your bike. Go a bit too speedily or seem to be pedalling with more than a moderate amount of passion and the police are perfectly within the law to pull you over for 'furious cycling'! Following an incident in 1790, when a coachman drove furiously at the Prince of Wales, such propulsion of any carriage has been officially forbidden. Chris Hoy, take note…

92. Double-Decker Digs

It's hard getting on the property ladder these days, particularly in Worcestershire's Upton-upon-Severn. There, married couples are expressly forbidden from living in a discarded bus. Presumably it's all right if you are still only engaged.

93. Well, I'll Be Blowed

Next time a London cabbie tootles you melodiously for some perceived slight of roadway etiquette, you might want to politely remind him that it is against the law to 'blow any horn' in the street, unless you are a postal worker. Alternatively, you might just want to respond in a less scholarly manner.

94. Roadkill Regulated

Bear in mind though, that it's perfectly legal for a vehicle driver to slaughter, gut and dress an animal in the streets of London – as long as he ran over it beforehand. Which is probably why the cabbie was driving so close in the first place.

95. She Charmed the Court

When a driver in the UK was given a parking penalty for leaving her car outside a building with the engine running, she challenged the fine. She claimed that her car had been full of snakes that she was going to use for a belly-dancing act. Not wanting the snakes to fall asleep in a cold car, she left the engine running to help them stay awake ready for the act. The adjudicator decided that was a legitimate defence and let the belly-dancing snake charmer wiggle out of paying the fine.

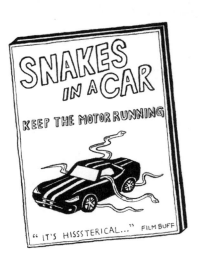

Death
Penalties

96. A Location to Die For

If you fancy a spot of eternal life, forget the Holy Grail; just go and live in the remote Arctic town of Longyearbyen, where dying is against the law. Actually, this is because it was found that bodies didn't decompose in the permafrost. The graveyard stopped accepting newcomers 70 years ago; so, if you fall gravely ill there now, you will be hastily dispatched by plane to the mainland, where you can end your days without getting arrested.

97. He Died for His Country

Although it's often thought that dying is illegal in the Houses of Parliament, this isn't strictly the case; kicking the bucket there is frowned upon rather than actually forbidden. This is because anyone who dies within the Palace of Westminster is technically entitled to a state funeral, which might tempt moribund attention-seekers to cark it in the visitors' bar just to get a spectacular send-off at the state's expense.

98. Suicide Bond

Even if you weren't sure of the lethal dose of drugs or were too timid to actually leap from Beachy Head, it was worth giving your suicide attempt a bash in England before 1961. The act was then a capital offence, so even if you buggered the whole thing up, the state could still hang you for even attempting it.

99. Where There's a Will There's a Wait

If you're going to the courts to contest a Will, be careful. Balasaheb Patloji Thorat of Poona in India decided to do just that, in 1205, when he was denied the rights of presiding over public functions and taking precedence at religious festivals. The lawsuit took a little longer than he expected. It was finally decided in favour of his descendant Maloji Thorat on 28 April 1966.

100. Mourning the Sandwich

Make sure you're full up on food before heading to a funeral in Massachusetts. In this East-Coast state, mourners at a wake may eat no more than three sandwiches each. The days of the gluttonous mourner are well and truly numbered.

101. Till Death Do Us Start

In 1959, the Malpasset Dam in southern France burst, claiming hundreds of lives. President de Gaulle visited the area and a young woman called Irène Jodard pleaded with him to allow her to continue with her marriage plans even though her fiancé had drowned. Later that month, a law allowing Ms Jodard to marry her deceased fiancé, André Capra, was drafted. Hundreds of bereft partners have applied for post-mortem matrimony since then. The question is: should such a bride wear white, or black?

102. Where There's a Will There's a Way

According to Britain's Wills Act 1837, a Will must be attested by witnesses 'in the presence of the testator'. You might think this is a clear enough definition, but no. In 1849 a Will was thrown out because, although the testator was in the room, his neck was too stiff to allow him to turn and see the actual signing. And in 1781, a testatrix decided it was too hot to come into the lawyer's office so she sat outside in her breezy carriage. Luckily it was decided that she could see enough of what was going on through the window. Try that next time you're at work on a sunny day.

The Game Is Up

103. The Urban Jungle

You are probably aware that cockfighting is illegal in the UK, and this is thanks to the Metropolitan Police Act 1839. It also outlaws bear- and badger-baiting. What is less well known is that this same statute still prevents you from 'fighting lions'. Just in case you were tempted to pop down to Soho and wrestle a giant jungle cat this weekend…

104. The Laws of the Game

The simplest ideas are the best. And lawmakers in Arizona came up with a genius solution to the problem of their hopeless college football team: legislate against the opposition. 'It shall be unlawful for any visiting football team or player to carry, convey, tote, kick, throw, pass, or otherwise transport or propel any inflated pigskin across the University of Arizona goal line or score a safety within the confines of the city of Tucson, County of Pima, State of Arizona.' That's pretty much got it covered, then.

105. Slip Slidin' up up and Away

We intuitively know that lawmakers are killjoys. But if you needed proof, here it is: the English courts can issue a £1,000 fine to 'every person who flies any kite, or who makes or uses any slide upon ice or snow'. But the key word here would seem to be 'or'; presumably a reasonably nit-picky lawyer could get you off for flying a kite while sliding on snow. 'Ice-kiting', anyone?

106. Golfers Driven Off

In 1491 King James IV of Scotland outlawed golf (and football) because the men of the country were spending too much time launching divots over the links when they should have been practising their archery. Of course, like much prohibition, this law simply drew people's attention to these sports, making them more popular than ever. Just 50 years later, golf was the favourite sport of the royalty – Mary Queen of Scots was very partial to a spot of putting. Before she lost her head, that is.

107. You're a Charming Chap, and You Know You Are

Be very careful what you call the football referee: under section 28 of the UK Town Police Clauses Act 1847 it is an offence (punishable by a £1,000 fine) 'to sing any profane or obscene song or ballad, or use any profane or obscene language', no matter how poor the ref's judgement may be. Or how blind he might seem.

108. A Hot Deal

In the UK, if you live 'within a mile of any arsenal or any store for explosives' you might expect to be forbidden from owning a few things that ordinary people take for granted – large barbecues, sky lanterns, fireworks, bazookas, and so on. But you wouldn't have thought that a pack of playing cards would be particularly dangerous, would you? But they're prohibited as well, so they must be.

Loopy Lawsuits

109. The Rock 'N' Roll Judge

When the song 'Barbie Girl' by Aqua hit the Top 40 in 1997, Mattel filed an infringement suit for the unfair use of the doll's name. Record company MCA contested Mattel's claims and countersued for defamation after Mattel had likened MCA to a bank robber. In 2002, a Court of Appeals ruled the song was protected as a parody under the First Amendment to the United States Constitution. The judge, Alex Kozinski, also threw out MCA's defamation lawsuit, concluding his ruling: 'The parties are advised to chill'.

110. Bonking Bonkers

Gloria Sykes moved to San Francisco in 1964, and had only been living in the city for two weeks when she was involved in a cable-car accident. She sued the cable-car company for damages; not for the physical injuries she sustained, but because the crash turned her from a devout Lutheran into a nymphomaniac. She claimed to have been unable to stop herself bedding hundreds of men – as many as 50 in one particular week. The court granted her $50,000 in compensation.

111. The Ultimate in Self-Storage

Wanda Hudson of Alabama was in her self-storage unit one evening when the storage facility manager locked her inside by mistake. Bizarrely, she didn't call for help or bang on the door and spent the next 63 days inside, living on the few edibles she kept in there. Barely alive by the end of the ordeal, she dropped from 150 pounds in weight to just 83 pounds. After recovering, she sued the storage yard for $10 million, claiming negligence. The jury awarded her $100,000, not having been told that Hudson had previously diagnosed mental problems. Although, in all fairness, they had probably guessed.

112. Life's a Drag

Ne'er-do-wells Jason Householder and John Stockum of Coshocton, Ohio, were convicted of criminal damages after being caught throwing beer bottles at a woman in a car in 2001. County Judge David Hostetler handed down an unusual sentence: the men could spend 60 days in jail or pay a $250 fine and walk through downtown Coshocton dressed as women for one hour. The two men chose the dresses, wigs and make-up. Their friends chose to line the route and laugh themselves silly.

113. Do as I Say, Not as I Do

Nancy Zelno of Philadelphia was fired from her teaching job for 'immoral conduct' after receiving her third conviction for drink driving. She sued her employer for wrongful termination, claiming that 'no students had been corrupted and her ability to teach hadn't been affected'. Her termination was upheld both by a tribunal and the state appeals court. The fact that her teaching post was at a drug and alcohol treatment clinic might have had something to do with this.

114. A Bad Break-Up

A man in Massachusetts sued his girlfriend because, he claimed, she broke his penis during a particularly creative sexual session. When the lissom lass tried a bold new manoeuvre, her boyfriend's penis simply folded. He sued her for damages for 'negligent sexual intercourse', which resulted with sexual dysfunction. The court decided that she was not liable because, even though the penis was clearly, er, dicked, the sex was consensual.

115. It's Tobacco, Not Toebacco

In the case of Pillars vs RJ Reynolds Tobacco Company in Mississippi in 1918, the following judgement was handed down: 'We can imagine no reason why, with ordinary care, human toes could not be left out of chewing tobacco, and if toes are found in chewing tobacco, it seems to us that somebody has been very careless'. Seems like somebody put their foot in it.

116. Robber Rewarded

In 2003, Richard Schick sued his former employer, the Illinois Department of Public Aid, for sexual and disability discrimination. A jury empathised with him and awarded him $303,830 in damages. Alas, the money didn't do him much good, as Schick had become so stressed-out by this discrimination that he'd held up a convenience store with a shotgun and was serving 10 years for armed robbery at the time of his claim. Still, he might have been able to avoid some discrimination in the prison showers.

117. Pennies From Heaven

There's nothing like an unforecasted shower for ruining your summer picnic. But when an Israeli TV station predicted good weather and it rained, one woman got so angry that she sued them. She claimed the errant forecast led her to dress lightly and so catch the flu in the downpour. She then missed a week of work and had to cough up for medication. Incredibly, she sued for US $1,000 and won. If that had happened in Britain, the BBC would have gone bust years ago.

118. Super-Sizzle Me

In 1992, 79-year-old Stella Liebeck from Albuquerque bought a coffee from a McDonald's drive-through. When she spilled the scalding drink in her own lap she sued McDonald's for negligence and won $160,000 in compensatory damages and a further $2.7 million in punitive damages. This might seem like the ultimate loopy lawsuit, but attorneys later revealed that McDonald's had ignored 700 previous injury claims about its coffee, which it then kept 20 degrees hotter than recommended; and Liebeck had been burned so severely that she was hospitalised for a week and needed several skin grafts. Good job she didn't get an apple pie as well.

119. Prison Sucks

Utah prison inmate Robert Paul Rice sued the Department of Corrections for not letting him practise his religion of 'Druidic Vampire'. Rice insisted that his religious rights included sexual access to a 'vampress' and 'vampiric dietary needs' (blood). The suit was thrown out because 1) records showed that Rice registered as a Catholic when imprisoned, and 2) everyone knows that if he had really been a vampire he could have just turned into a bat and flown out of prison at night.

120. The Case of the Pre-Loved Pants

A London man once bought a pair of underpants from a department store and wore them without washing them first. He later realised that he had pubic lice. He deduced that someone had tried the pants on at the shop before him, and he had picked up the lice from the underwear. (At least, that's what he told his wife.) He sued the shop, but the court decided that a reasonable person would wash their underwear before wearing it, so he lost. If he appealed, he definitely should have changed briefs.

121. Breast Defence

P aul Shimkonis from Florida sued his local pole-dancing club in 1996, claiming to have suffered whiplash caused by a lap-dancer's large breasts. Poor Paul reported the bounteous bosoms hit him like 'cement blocks', causing him physical harm and mental anguish. He sought reparations to the tune of $15,000, but the judge bounced his claim out of court.

122. Man Vs Himself

In 1995, prisoner Robert Lee Brock sued himself. He claimed he had violated his own civil rights and religious beliefs when he allowed himself to get drunk. And, since it was while inebriated that he committed his crimes, he demanded $5 million from himself for the stress and inconvenience of getting himself incarcerated. However, since he didn't earn an income behind bars, he felt the state of Virginia should pay. The judge threw the case straight out, and Brock straight back into his cell.

123. Beer Goggles Broken

In 1991, Richard Overton sued Anheuser-Busch, brewers of Budweiser, for $10,000. The beer's ad campaign at the time showed two beautiful women coming to life in front of truck drivers. Overton claimed to have suffered emotional distress, mental injury and financial loss because drinking Bud didn't make gorgeous girls magically materialise before him. The case was dismissed. Presumably he'd drunk a few cans when he filed the claim, too.

124. The Damage is Dung

In 1928, a young lady attended a circus performance in Georgia, USA. According to testimony later given in a lawsuit, she was seated in the front row when 'a horse, which was going through a dancing performance immediately in front of where the plaintiff was sitting, ... caused to back towards the plaintiff, and while in this situation the horse evacuated his bowels into her lap, that this occurred in full view of many people, ... all of whom laughed at the occurrence, that as a result thereof the plaintiff was caused much embarrassment, mortification, and mental pain and suffering...' The court found in favour of the plaintiff.

125. Oh, for God's Sake

A Minnesota man named Christopher Roller sued David Blaine and David Copperfield, in 2005, demanding that they reveal the secrets of their magic tricks to him. Oh, and that they give him 10 per cent of their total income – for life – as well. Why? It's simple: Roller believes that the magicians are defying the laws of physics, and so are using godly powers – not actionable in itself, you might think. Ah, but you see, Roller believes that he himself is God, and therefore it is his powers that the magicians are stealing.

126. Oh Deer, Oh Deer

P ETA, the right-on animal rights crew, held an anti-deerhunting protest, in 2001, which went jolly well until two protestors knocked down a deer on the way home. Their minds obviously irreparably boggled with guilt at bashing Bambi's brains out, they promptly sued the New Jersey Division of Fish and Wildlife for damages 'as a result of their deer management program, which includes, in certain circumstances, an affirmative effort to increase deer population'. Erm…?

127. Hex Factor

Back in 1901, an Iowa singing group called the Cherry Sisters sued the *Des Moines Register* for reviewing their act thus: 'Their long skinny arms, equipped with talons at the extremities, swung mechanically, and anon waved frantically at the suffering audience. The mouths of their rancid features opened like caverns, and sounds like the wailing of damned souls issued therefrom.' A cast-iron case of libel, surely? But the judge decided that he really ought to attend a performance before ruling. He did, and immediately found for the paper.

128. Plod's Ponging Paws

A 1937 advertisement in Britain showed a sweaty policeman mopping his brow with the headline, 'Phew, I'm going to get my feet into a Jeyes Fluid footbath'. But the advertising agency hadn't got the policeman's permission to use the image; so he sued, claiming the ad made him seem 'slovenly and unclean'. The advertisers didn't roll over – they forced him to admit in court that a hard-working policeman's feet would indeed benefit from a soak in Jeyes Fluid. But he insisted this would only be because they ached, not because they ponged. He won £100 in damages.

129. A Low Blow

Poor Stewart Blair was fixing a snowplough blade in Wisconsin in 1994, with his friend Maurice Poulin, when he slipped, fell and sustained some nasty injuries. Seeking redress he duly filed a lawsuit – but not against the blade manufacturer or even the council's road department. He sued his pal, claiming Mr Poulin had caused his accident – by farting in his face. The jury retired for 3 hours to have a good laugh, then threw the suit out.

130. Smell the Money

While we're on this odorous topic, we should point out that, while blowing off in someone's face might not get you hauled before the bailiff, calling someone a noxious name could very well do – at least in the US. A former manager of the cafeteria at Washington's Smithsonian Museum won $400,000 in damages because his boss called him an 'old fart'.

I'm Glad You Warned Me

131. Flagging it Up

In January 1941, before the United States joined World War II, two protesting US Navy sailors tore down a Nazi flag flying from the German consulate in San Francisco. They were arrested, tried, and convicted of malicious mischief. The American flag gets even greater protection – the state of Washington has passed a law stating that it is illegal to paint polka dots on the Stars and Stripes. Where that state stands on polka-dotted swastikas is not clear.

132. Is That a Snapper in Your Pocket or Are You Just Pleased to See Me?

It's tough being an electrician in Austin, Texas: you cannot carry wire cutters in your pocket. The statutes seem also to be loaded against farmers in Wichita, Kansas, where it is illegal to carry a concealed bean-snapper. Mind you, for all we know, a bean-snapper could be either a tool, or some sort of dwarf crocodile, so that might be an entirely sensible ruling.

133. The Daily Liar

In Oklahoma, it is illegal to print lies in a newspaper to increase sales. This differs somewhat from the custom in the UK, of course, where doing so is virtually compulsory.

134. Nabbed for Napping

Be careful to ensure your bath isn't too soothing if you're staying in Detroit. There, sleeping in the bath could really get you in to hot water. They're a bit more practical in Pittsburgh, where the household appliance you're not allowed to sleep in is the fridge. While in Lubbock, Texas, you face a fine if you crash out in a trash can. Which must be why Officer Dibble got so upset with Top Cat.

135. Are You Taking the OAP?

It is against the law to impersonate one of London's Chelsea Pensioner's. It's also not that funny. Mind you, this law seems to have come about because the old rogues were getting up to mischief: the same act insists that all linen at the veterans' home is stamped with the name of the Chelsea Hospital so that they can't sell their bed sheets. Although, the question of who was buying the used linen from an OAP's home is surely more troubling.

136. Thai Him Up

Thailand may tolerate many exotic sexual shenanigans, but it is still illegal to leave your house there if you are not wearing underwear. And you can't drive your car if you're not wearing a shirt, no matter what's going on in your trousers. Nor should you step on any of the nation's currency. And don't even think of insulting the king – you could get 15 years in jail. Just stick to the ladyboys and you'll be fine.

137. A Tooth for a Tooth

An edict in Yukon, Oklahoma, forbids patients from pulling out their dentists' teeth, no matter how sorely they are tempted. The same is true in South Foster, Rhode Island; but if a dentist there plucks out a wrong tooth, the patient can order the village blacksmith to extract the corresponding gnasher from the dentist's mouth. Whether this should be with the benefit of a hammer-based anaesthetic is not specified.

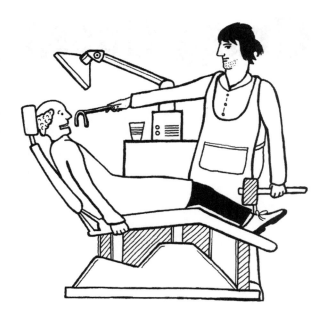

Crazy Cases

138. Mum's the Word

When you leave a Will as short and sweet as 'All to mother', as a Mr Dickens did in 1906, you might think there could be no legal comeback. However, this Will was successfully contested, for a very good reason: Dickens's mother was long dead. It transpired that the deceased fellow was in the habit of calling his wife 'mother' (as in 'mother of his children') and had somehow neglected to clarify this in his Will.

139. In the Lap of the Gods

Women in Washington who sit on men's laps on buses or on trains, without placing a pillow under their posteriors, face six months in jail. The authorities there probably heard about Richard Plant from Johannesburg, who was naked from the waist down when arrested by traffic cops. He claimed that his nudity was actually being hidden from the public by his girlfriend, who was helpfully sitting on his lap at the time. The jury laughed so much that they had to let him off.

140. The Letter of he Law

The law is notoriously nit-picky – and sometimes this can work in favour of the accused. In 1823, Thomas Halloway was charged in Hereford, UK, with pinching 'a brass furnace'. However, the stealing had been done in neighbouring Radnor and, by the time Halloway had returned home, he'd cut the furnace up. He was freed because he didn't have a stolen brass furnace in Hereford, just 'pieces of brass'. Another man was charged with stealing 'a pair of stockings', but got off when his counsel pointed out he had nicked two odd ones. Similarly, a thief was found not guilty of pinching a duck when it was pointed out that the bird up his jumper was a drake. It's completely quackers, really.

141. Standing Up for His Rights

Florida banned 'dwarf tossing' – contests to see who could throw a dwarf across a bar for the furthest distance – in 1989. Shortly after, David Flood, a radio presenter in Tampa, challenged this statute in the US District Court. Flood, also known as 'Dave the Dwarf', claimed that the ban was unconstitutional and he should be allowed to decide for himself whether to participate in the barroom contests. Flood stated his legal position: 'Just because I'm 3-foot-2 doesn't mean I can't make decisions. I'm a dwarf and I want to be tossed.'

142. Taking the Law Into his Own Hands

Usually, British legal deeds conclude with the words 'signed by my hand'. 'Aha!' thought one enterprising merchant, in 1652, who faced the minor problem that the person he wanted to sign his deed was dead. He simply chopped off the chap's hand, stuck a pen in it and signed the document with that. The court didn't approve of his handiwork – he was fined £100 and put in the pillory.

Royal
Rules

143. The Defence Calls the Queen of England

Can you put the British monarch in the witness box? Well, when the Duke of Buckingham was impeached in 1626, he called Charles I in his defence. This put the lawyers in a proper tizzy – prosecutions are done in the name of the Crown, making the sovereign the source of justice itself. The King's evidence could therefore never be questioned. But since he couldn't be prosecuted for perjury if he lied, his testimony would technically be worthless. Charles got around this paradox by dissolving Parliament and having Buckingham tried in the Star Chamber, where he was let off. However, the matter has never been satisfactorily resolved, and it may still be legally possible to call the Queen to court.

144. Who Let the Dogs Out?!

Canine social climbing is officially outlawed in the UK: 'the severest Penaltys will be suffered by any commoner who doth permit his animal to have carnal knowledge of a pet of the Royal House'. So states a law laid down in the reign of George I. So, if your pooch has a passion for corgis, you'd better make sure that he or she is always on a lead when you go visiting the royal palaces.

145. My Fairy King

I t might seem like England's Henry III was a very sensible lawmaker: in 1225, he revised the Magna Carta of his father, King John, and it was Henry's more concise version that was later enshrined in statute. However, since he also enacted a law decreeing the death penalty for anyone found killing, wounding or maiming fairies, he goes down as a happy pioneer of the English reputation for barking-mad regulation.

146. Royal Unrobing

The English Treason Act of 1351 made it quite clear that if you 'violate the King's companion, or the king's eldest daughter unmarried, or the wife of the King's eldest son' you are committing treason. And, technically, this offence carried the death penalty until 1998; until which year anybody philandering with the aforementioned royals could have been beheaded or burned at the stake. Not that any of their gracious majesties would ever engage in such activities…

147. Friends in Low Places

It is also considered treason in the UK to burn down a brothel. A gang of boys was convicted and executed for just such an offence in 1663, after trying to demolish a 'disorderly house'. The Old Bailey Chief Justice indicted them for 'levying war'; a charge that he said applied not just to a body of people gathered as an army, but any company grouped together in public. 'If this thing is to be endured,' the Justice said, 'who is safe?' Presumably not his legal colleagues who had witnessed the attack from within the brothel itself.

148. Off with Her Majesty's Head

When England had no monarch in the 17th century interregnum, an Act of Parliament made it high treason for a person to take the 'name, style, dignity, power, prerogative or authority of King of England and Ireland'. This act was never repealed, so the restored Charles II was technically breaking it. Our own Queen Elizabeth II is doing the same – legally she is a traitor who ought to be locked up. Until 1973 she could even have been beheaded. What are the police waiting for?

149. Going for the Natural Look

It's all very right and proper that girls should be bewitching. Unless you're Elizabeth I, that is, and it's your job to be the most captivating woman in the land. Which is presumably why Good Queen Bess outlawed women enticing men into marriage by using make-up, wigs, false hips or high heels – under penalty of being tried for witchcraft. Jealous much, your Majesty?

150. A Net Loss

In 1324, Edward II decreed that whales and sturgeon caught or washed up on British coastline must be offered to the Crown. So when Robert Davies caught a 120kg sturgeon in 2004, he loyally faxed Buckingham Palace and was told to 'dispose of it as he saw fit'. He naturally decided that the best way to do this was by selling it for £650 – and that's when the police nabbed him. Even with royal consent, it is still illegal to sell the fish. The Crown may have made the rules, but it can't break them.

151. Long Live the King! Long Live the King, Again!

The Regency Act 1830 established the curious law that a princess or other heir can succeed twice to the British throne. The first time would be when the old king died and his widow had no son; his daughter or other heir would be crowned. If the widow then gave birth to the dead king's son, this youth would be king, displacing the older sibling or other heir. However, if that new king later died without issue, then the crown would revert back to the original heir.

152. Buried Treasure

It is a long-observed convention, if not an actual law, that the British Crown should not leave the country. This is normally good for security purposes, but it threatened to become a nightmare in the darkest days of World War II, when the royal regalia couldn't be taken overseas for safekeeping. In the end, the Crown Jewels were buried in a spot the whereabouts of which only three people knew. That's about as good an excuse for avoiding conscription as you could hope for.

153. A Touch Too Much

S ection 4 of the Royal Parks and Other Open Spaces Regulations 1997 states that 'touching a pelican' is expressly forbidden, unless you have prior written permission, of course presumably from the park-keeper, rather than the pelican. It's also illegal to wash your linen in the Serpentine, no matter how tempting it might seem. Nor should you 'interfere with a fungus'. Just let it be.

Clothing... and the Lack Thereof

154. Goddess on a Highway

Forget protest marches or sports matches – when it comes to public order the big danger for many lawmakers is women's swimwear. Especially in Kentucky, where: 'No female shall appear in a bathing suit on any highway within the Commonwealth of Kentucky unless she be escorted by at least two officers or unless she be armed with a club'. An amendment clarifies that this doesn't apply to 'females weighing less than 90 pounds nor exceeding 200 pounds nor shall it apply to female horses'. Obviously.

155. G.I. No

If you're one of those spirited sorts who relaxes by re-enacting battles, you might want to think twice about taking a Caribbean holiday – it's against the law to wear camouflage clothing in Trinidad and Tobago. Apparently this is to prevent people from imitating military and other officials, and you can be detained and have your camo kit confiscated. That is, of course, if they can find you.

156. She Made a Splash

In March 2000, while holidaying in Mexico, Amber Kulhanek had a few drinks and was videotaped taking her top off in a wet t-shirt contest. When her image later appeared on a 'Wild Party Girls' video ad, she filed a $5-million lawsuit. Amber claimed that the embarrassment of friends and family seeing the commercial showing her bare breasts caused her to drop out of college. She won when the defendant didn't turn up for the hearing.

157. The Thong Arm of the Law

Macrida Patterson, a 52-year-old traffic cop from Los Angeles, recently sued the Victoria's Secret underwear company for damage to her eye. The injury happened when she was trying on a new thong. The garment was so tight-fitting that a metal clip pinged off and half-blinded her. Lawyers have taken down her particulars.

158. Bare-Chested About-Face

The Swinging Sixties saw an explosion of go-go dancers in clubs, much to the particular annoyance of Birmingham City Council. Those righteous representatives duly passed a bylaw forcing 'all go-go dancers' to wear bras while performing. They were later forced to amend this following a celebrated burst of on-stage cross-dressing. A humbled spokesman said: 'no male go-go dancer will hereafter have to wear a brassiere'.

159. The Naked City... 1

In Georgia it is illegal to change the clothes on a shop mannequin unless the blinds are down. In New York you are free to change the clothes – and indeed leave the mannequin standing there naked – unless it's night-time. Then it's against the law and a good thing too – who knows what the sight of an unclothed plastic dummy would cause the sane, law-abiding people who frequent Manhattan in the wee hours to do?

160. The Naked City... 2

The city of Liverpool is another place with a bee in its legal bonnet about artificial nudity. There, shop assistants will be breaking the law if they 'dress or undress a female mannequin in the window of any store or shop where children might observe the unclothed model'. And any children caught peering up the dress of a mannequin will get their parents arrested. Which is actually a pretty smart way of escaping from any more shopping.

161. Barefaced Cheek

If you're on a safari in Kenya and your guide suddenly removes all of his clothes before wandering off towards the wildlife, do resist the temptation to do the same. While it's completely legal for Kenyan citizens to streak across the Masai Mara, it is illegal for foreigners to do so. It's also deeply inadvisable for at least 147 other reasons.

162. Poker-Faced

There's a reason why Lady Gaga has never played a gig in Charlotte, North Carolina: the law there states that all women must cover their bodies with a minimum of 16 yards of cloth. However, the artist's famous raw-meat dress would go down a storm in Helena, Montana, where females performing in nightclubs and taverns must wear 'no less than 3 pounds 2 ounces of clothing'.

163. That Dress Is Smoking Hot

In Schulter, Oklahoma, it is a misdemeanour if any woman plays a game of chance or gambles while 'in the nude, dressed in revealing and sheer clothing or while wrapped in a towel'. Which kind of takes all the fun out of strip poker. However, in St Louis, women must be fully dressed before they can be rescued by a firefighter. Which surely takes some of the fun out of being a firefighter.

164. You'll Have Someone's Eye out With That

Fans of modern millinery should avoid New Jersey: 'any person who shall wear in a public place any device or thing attached to her head, hair, headgear or hat, which device is capable of lacerating the flesh of any other person with whom it may come in contact and which is not sufficiently guarded against the possibility of so doing, shall be adjudged a disorderly person'. Which is a shame, because strimmer-brims are so in this year.

165. Hat Hysterics

In 1797, James Heatherington appeared in London wearing the first top hat, and was fined £50 by the Lord Mayor for 'appearing on the public highway, wearing upon his head a tall structure, having a shining lustre and calculated to frighten timid people'. It seems unusual that hats have always incurred judges' wrath, which is ironic considering they have a doormat made of bleached horsehair draped over their own noggins.

166. No Need to Pack Your PJs

The owner of every hotel in Hastings, Nebraska, is required by law to provide each guest with a clean and pressed nightshirt. Furthermore, no couple, even if they are married, may sleep together in the nude; nor may they have sex – unless they are wearing one of these clean, white cotton nightshirts. Which, unless you have a thing for shapeless cotton nightwear, is hardly likely to put you in the mood anyway.

167. Keeping Abreast of the Law

Usually, nudity is on the receiving end of stiff legal strictures. However, England's James I passed what can best be described as a 'Topless Act'. This decreed that all maidens appearing in public should have their breasts exposed as far as the nipple. In the 16th century this was a true symbol of their virginity. The fact that James I became a hugely popular king who achieved political unity and oversaw the flowering of a cultural 'Golden Age' is probably just a coincidence.

168. Pranksters on Parade

Taking your clothes off in public is indecent exposure – unless you are in Whitehaven, Cumbria. There, women are uniquely allowed to walk around the town – not just the beach – with bare breasts. And, although streaking at sports events is technically a no-no, the Home Office Committee has ruled that 'streakers are looked upon as no more than relatively innocent pranksters… able to avoid any stigma or a conviction'.

169. Caped Commuters

Hat-loving city girls beware – an Act from 1611 that is still in force forbids female workers in the City of London from wearing on their heads any item made from 'cambric, tiffiny or linen cloth' worth more than 5 shillings a foot. Also out are farthingales – hoops that expand your hipline – and silk aprons, silk stockings and Spanish-leather shoes. Your penalty if caught is a fine of 3s 4d (about £16 today). You are, however, allowed to wear velvet capes.

170. (Don't) Show Us a Leg

Girls, be careful this summer if you're in St Peters, the village at the heart of Broadstairs in Kent. For there you are forbidden by law from showing your ankles in public. Such slutty deviancy could still, technically, get you put in the village stocks.

The Bizarre at the Bar

171. Our Appeal is Knackered

You can't consent to assault. In 1994, a man decided that getting his lover to nail his foreskin to a plank would be a jolly idea. The police disagreed and the men were convicted. Appealing under Article 8 of the European Convention on Human Rights, which guarantees respect for private life, they said they'd both consented to the act itself; the wood, the nails, the hammer (and the private parts) belonged to them and so they could do what they like. They lost.

172. Love Letters

however, in 1997, a Mr Wilson was convicted of actual bodily harm in the UK for branding his initials on his wife's buttocks at her request. Feeling that he'd got a bum rap, he went to the Court of Appeal where Lord Justice Russell criticised the decision to bring the case to trial at all. He triumphantly ruled in favour of Mr Wilson, saying: 'Mrs Wilson not only consented to that which the appellant did, she insisted on it'.

173. A Tall Tail

The people of former Yugoslavia once got so irate at the presence of Halley's comet in the night sky that they outlawed it. The interplanetary ball of frozen rock and gas then showed admirable restraint for 74 years before losing all control and blazing a fiery trail across the Balkan skies once more. Unfortunately, there is no surviving record of who was sent to arrest it.

174. Out of This World

According to the brilliantly named 'The Outer Space Act 1986', the Secretary of State is permitted to use 'reasonable force' to prevent an alien invasion of the UK – as long as the aliens don't possess a licence to invade. In which case, they can operate their 'space objects' in perfect legality. This is the sort of law that truly made Britain great.

175. I Don't Have the Heart to Fine You

Dr Frank Pantridge was a brilliant cardiologist who invented the portable defibrillator. This life-saving innovation earned him the freedom of his home town (Hillsborough in Northern Ireland). One ancient legal right of this honour is that of driving his sheep anywhere in town. Dr Pantridge owned no sheep, but he did stick lots of pictures of them to his car windows so that he could park wherever he fancied. Cheeky, but he was so beloved by the town that he never got a ticket.

176. Not Feeling Very Flush

You must plan your movements very carefully in Switzerland. Flushing the toilet after 10pm in an apartment building is illegal there. The Government curiously considered noise pollution to be more anti-social than olfactory pollution. Not sure we agree with them on that one. Anyway, whether you relieve yourself and leave the flat humming, or you just wait until morning, the choice is completely yours.

177. Zombies Have Rights Too

New Jersey is the most zombie-friendly place on earth: hunting is prohibited in Mountain View Cemetery. However, the state also forbids you from carrying a lunchbox down Main Street (whether it's full of brains or not) so any hungry undead are advised to eat at home before they go lurching around the town.

178. Going out With a Bang – or Not

If the nuclear warning sounded, what would you do? Yep, and so would everyone else in the world – apart from the good people of Utah. There, alcohol may not be sold during an emergency. And no one may have sex in the back of an ambulance if it's responding to an emergency call; so that's that one out, too. However, you ought not find yourself in such a situation in the first place, since state law decrees that it is illegal to detonate any nuclear weapon.

179. L'injunction Très Super

Injunctions are all the rage these days, but the sort brought by frisky footballers costs a packet. In the Channel Islands, however, you can get one simply by dropping to one knee, baring your head and shouting, 'Haro, haro, haro, à l'aide, mon prince, on me fait tort'. (Hear ye, hear ye, hear ye, come to my aid, my Prince, I am being wronged.) Then just recite the Lord's Prayer in French, and the local courts will have to hear your complaint. Originally a way of summoning help to the victim of a crime, it was used during a property dispute as recently as 2010.

180. Basket Case

You are not allowed to sell baskets in the City of London. Since this order was enacted by Edward IV, in response to a fire in 1538 in the basket-makers' quarter that killed nine people, it presumably refers to the wicker type. But perhaps a case could be made for the baskets of financial products that frazzled the economy. They're far more dangerous than a two-tone laundry hamper.

181. Miaow!

In Australia it is illegal to roam the streets wearing black clothes and felt shoes while wearing black shoe polish on your face, as these are widely recognised as being the accoutrements of a cat burglar. In the state of Victoria, you are also not allowed to wear pink hot pants on a Sunday after midday. Cat burglars are a bit funkier in Victoria, it seems.

182. Mandatory Mid-Atlantic Monikers

One of the best things about being a rock star is being able to show off your creative wackiness by calling your new baby 'Cherry-Pie Bumfluff' or something similar. But such New Age naming is illegal in Iceland. To protect the island's heritage you must choose your child's moniker from a Government-approved list of Icelandic names. However, half of these are Björking mad anyway, so there's still plenty of scope for creative Christening.

183. One Desires a Sahssage Sammich

Speaking English is illegal in Illinois, thanks to author HL Mencken who, in 1919, had 'American' declared the official state language. This seems strange – until you go to Chicago. The Queen's English sure ain't what they talkin' over by dere…

184. Bearded Youth

Teenagers may think they have it tough growing up in today's Western Society. But it's a breeze compared with life in Malagasy Indian tribes, in which it's the 'up' part of growing up that is the problem – a young man must pay his father for the right to grow taller than him. And, as long as his father is alive, he cannot shave or eat animal rumps. Shaving animal rumps is probably okay, though.

185. Wiping the Record Clean

You can write a cheque on anything that's portable, as long as the item carries details of your account, the date, the payee and the amount on it, together with your signature. This was proved in Canada during the 1930s, when a farmer painted a cheque on the side of a cow and cashed it. Britain's Dick Roper went one step further and paid a £30 parking ticket with a cheque written on toilet paper. He admitted that he was sorely tempted to use it first.

186. I Wondered What That Teddy Was Doing There...

In Denmark, you legally have to check under your car for children who may be sleeping there before you start the engine. But don't panic too much if you forget and get thrown in jail for running over some catnapping kids – in Denmark it is not against the law to escape from prison.

187. Nothing Shocks a Belgian

Walt Disney: wholesome family entertainer or public nuisance? Well, he's been thought to be the latter in many places, such as Romania, in 1935, where Mickey Mouse was banned in case he scared young children. At the other extreme, Belgium is the only country in the world to never impose any censorship laws on adult films. Which is nice (and naughty) to know.

Disorder in Court

188. How to Make a Clean Getaway

The world is a bit of a mess when it comes to laws on cleanliness. In Hungary, spring cleaning was made compulsory in 1937. Whereas in England, hanging washing in the street and beating a carpet are both punishable by a fine of £1,000. In San Francisco, you can beat the bejesus out of your rug between midnight and 8am, but don't even think about trying to sweep it. That could get you carpeted before a judge.

189. In Your Face, Buddy

'It is disorderly conduct for one man to greet another on the street by placing the end of his thumb against the tip of his nose, at the same time extending and wriggling the fingers of his hand.' Surely this is a law from the most civil spot on earth – Cambridge, perhaps, Harrogate or Frinton-on-Sea? Actually, this sort of riotous rudeness would get you arrested in New York.

190. Hair Bare Bunch

The smooth-chested look may be in for men, but you'll have to do it yourself in Omaha, Nebraska – the city's barbers are prohibited from shaving a man's torso. The same is true in Morrisville, Pennsylvania, but the law is even keener there – men must get a permit to shave themselves. Although, at least the town isn't sexist in its severity – the womenfolk of Morrisville need a permit to wear make-up, too.

191. For the Chop

Teachers in Arkansas who wear their hair in a bob face an expensive lesson – they will forfeit their annual pay rise. Bald men seeking luxuriant new locks should avoid New York – having your hair regrown is illegal there. While, if the hairdresser's scissors make your child nervous, you could consider going to Elkhart, Indiana, where barbers are specifically prohibited from threatening to cut off a child's ears. Which will make them feel so much better.

192. Bangs to Rights

If you think that's bad, you probably ought to avoid holidaying in Tanzania. Men there must keep their hair shorter than two inches and women can't wear too much make-up, or wigs. Get caught and you'll have your head shorn and your bottom warmed with four strokes of the cane. Miss another barbershop appointment, and you can be banged up for anything from six months to life. It's probably fair to say that the hippy movement was not particularly big in Tanzania.

193. What You Bin up To?

Mind you, in Seattle, it's Dibble who could get dobbed in: there, you can't remove the lids of a garbage can without the owner's permission – whether you are looking for a misbehaving cat in a purple waistcoat, or not. In New Orleans, it's the kicking of bins that is the problem; while in Montgomery, Alabama, you are forbidden from sitting on one, even if you are tired from a day of alley-cat antics.

194. Local Justice

Don't drop litter in Hammond, Indiana – you'll be forced to down a hefty dose of castor oil by the local cops. Mind you, that's slightly better than double parking in Minneapolis – the official punishment for that is to work on a chain gang on a diet of bread and water. In Turkey, the police can take drink drivers up to 20 miles outside town and force them to walk back. Presumably to their car – not the pub.

195. New Harrumphshire

Be careful about picking up someone else's litter in a park in New Hampshire. You might think that you're being a good citizen, but if you get caught collecting rubbish, raking sand or picking up seaweed, you may be fined $150 for 'maintaining the national forest without a permit'. Since the same state forbids you from tapping your feet, nodding your head or in any way keeping time to the music playing in a tavern, restaurant or café, you might want to think about holidaying elsewhere in the first place.

Property and Theft

196. Back to the Future

It's a quirk of Irish land law that leases lasting 'for ever' are quite frequently signed. There is a plot for a sewage tank adjoining Columb Barracks in Mullingar, County Westmeath, that has a lease for 10,000,000 years. As it was signed on 3 December 1868, this means that a future lawyer is expected to bring the agreement up for review in AD 10001868.

197. It Fell off the Back of a Handcart

The 'Market Overt Rules' were laid down in 1189 to oversee England's outdoor markets. They quirkily decreed that anything you bought from a market stall between sunrise and sunset was your legal property – even if it later turned out that the object had been stolen. Understandably, the Rules were informally known as the 'Thieves Charter', and were only abolished in 1995. Is it any wonder that Del Boy left our screens shortly after?

198. Arcane Arcade

The exclusive shopping precinct of Burlington Arcade in central London has its own unique laws, enforced by beadles in Edwardian frock coats and top hats. Obviously, shoplifting is out, but so too are the heinous crimes of humming, singing, hurrying, whistling and 'behaving boisterously'. Until relatively recently you weren't even allowed to carry a parcel within its hallowed halls. But then some bright spark realised that this would stop people buying anything bigger than a ham sandwich, and the law was brought bang up to date.

199. Sharp Practice

Every October, the City Solicitor for the City of London Corporation legally has to pay rent for a bit of land that the Corporation rented in Shropshire 700 years ago. Fair enough, if someone was still using it, but no one has known exactly where the bit of land is for several hundred years now. Good job the rent demanded is only one sharp axe and one blunt billhook. The City also has to shell out 61 nails and 6 horseshoes for a forge on the Strand that hasn't existed since 1235. It's a wonder how they afford it.

200. No Taxation Without Prosecution

If you've ever tried to squirm your way out of paying your council tax, you can sympathise with the residents of Corpus Christi in Texas, who, in 1980, thought they had the perfect scam. They simply voted in favour of a proposition to lower the local property tax ceiling and limit annual tax increases. The city authority watched as the locals patted one another on the back, then promptly sued them to recover their lost revenue, forcing the taxpayers to foot the bill for the lawsuit against themselves.

201. Bad Bards

honouring a literary celebrity by naming a street after them can backfire when the writer drifts from memory. But surely some heroes have proven their worth over the centuries? Not in Great Yarmouth. There, it is forbidden to name any streets after Chaucer, Milton, Byron, Tennyson, Shakespeare or any other poet. The reason given by the town council is: 'the moral character of these people is not such that we should name roads after them'. Although writers of prose are okay, of course – there is a Dickens Avenue in town.

202. Keep off the Grass – Seriously

Burn marks from your disposable barbecue could incur more than the wrath of the Parkie; they could also get you arrested. The UK Inclosure Act 1857 states you can be fined if you 'wilfully lay any manure, soil, ashes, or rubbish, or other matter or thing thereon, or do any other act whatsoever to the injury of such town or village green or land, or to the interruption of the use or enjoyment thereof as a place for exercise and recreation'. And don't drive your cattle onto it either.

203. Are You Telling Me Porkies, Sir?

Your front garden may look like a pigsty, but if that's because you actually keep pigs in it then you can expect a visit from… the Pigs. It is expressly forbidden by the UK's Town Police Clauses Act 1847 to keep any form of 'pigstye' facing onto the street, unless it is shut out by a large wall or fence.

204. Daylight Robbery

In these tough economic times, it's worth knowing that bailiffs in England and Wales don't have total carte blanche to enter your home and get their mucky mitts on your Wii. A bailiff is not allowed to break down your outer door to get in, but he can tell any sort of lie (such as pretending to be your mother-in-law) or trick (shouting that your house is on fire) to get you to open up. He can then kick in any inner door and, even if you manage to throw him out, he can then break back in again. Some sort of mantrap in the vestibule is probably the answer, for both bailiffs and mothers-in-law.

205. Don't Blow It

Ambitious vacuum-cleaner salesmen beware – you aren't allowed to attempt to sell one to a woman in a public place in the UK, no matter how much of a sucker she looks. If you're caught, you could get three months in jail. Of course, this means that the sales floor of Comet must count as a private place. So, presumably, it's legal to do anything you like with your vacuum there.

206. King of the Squatters

In Texas, an old law of 'adverse possession' states that if you occupy someone else's land for a period of time with the intention of dispossessing the true owner, you get the land. It originally helped squatters who were farming on land not owned by them. But, in 2011, when Kenneth Robinson moved into a $330,000 house in foreclosure, he filed the necessary paperwork with Denton County courthouse and paid a mere $16 for the rights to the house.

Religious Regulation

207. Eggs-Straordinary

In AD 325, Easter was defined as the first Sunday after the full moon following the vernal equinox. This means it hops around the calendar. To pin it down a bit, the UK's Easter Act 1928 established Easter Sunday as the Sunday following the second Saturday in April. Alas, Parliament had neglected to check whether the world's Christian churches would agree to the move. They didn't. And so, although this law was passed, it has never been implemented.

208. Sorry Love, God Told Me To Do It

When God passed Moses the Ten Commandments he laid down an eminently respectable and sensible set of laws. Er, not according to a Bible published in 1631, by the royal printers in London. The printers made a tiny but absolutely spectacular mistake: omitting a single word in Exodus 20:14, so that the Seventh Commandment read 'Thou shalt commit adultery'. They were fined £300 (£33,800 today) and lost their licence. This edition became known as *The Wicked Bible*.

209. It's the Way I Preach 'Em

No vicar likes a snoozy congregation, but they have to be wary of being too entertaining. In Kentucky, 'Any person who displays, handles or uses any kind of reptile in connection with any religious service or gathering shall be fined not less than 50 dollars...' While in Alabama it is illegal to wear a false moustache in church if it makes people laugh. And in Nicholas County, West Virginia, no clergy members may tell jokes or even humorous stories from the pulpit during church services. Another state law forbids snoozing on a train but says nothing about churches, which is handy considering the dull state of the sermons.

210. Divine Dress Code

Manchester once had a bylaw that forced all city councillors to go to church on Sunday. But the county of Somerset took things much more seriously. A law there stipulated that churchgoers had to wear completely different clothes on Sunday than they did during the rest of the week. Did the vicar check their pants, though? That's the burning question.

211. Holy Matrimony

Discrimination in the workplace is mostly illegal now – but not in the Church of England. If you are thinking of being ordained as a deacon, you had better hope your parents were married before you were born: you must be able to prove you're not a bastard if you want the job. If history is against you in this matter, you can apply to the Archbishop of Canterbury for a dispensation, and deaconship will be open to you. But you will never rise to the rank of bishop.

212. Prime and Prejewdice

Some laws promote equality, but a few still protect prejudice. One of the British Prime Minister's jobs is to help select the next Archbishop of Canterbury – unless the Prime Minister is Jewish. Then the Jews Relief Act 1858 kicks in and forbids him from advising on any ecclesiastical post. There's no problem if he or she's a Muslim, Sikh, Buddhist or even an atheist. In Conwy in North Wales, Jews are still outright forbidden from dwelling in the borough – at least, according to the ancient city charter.

213. The Original 'Bah Humbug'gers

In early 17th-century England, the 12 days of Christmas were fully and joyously celebrated with the country virtually shutting down for merriment. This irked influential Puritan politicians, who increasingly saw Christmas as an indulgent, Popish festival with no biblical justification. So, in 1644, they outlawed Christmas festivities. Three years later the Long Parliament abolished the feasts of Easter and Whitsun as well. The Easter bunny must have been a right troublemaker in those days…

214. Saucy Sabbath

Before Sunday trading was allowed, the Shops Act 1950 kept the Sabbath special in the UK. It stipulated what you could and couldn't buy and carried the threat of a £25 fine. It was a particularly asinine piece of legislation because one of the things you specifically couldn't buy was a Bible. Whereas you were perfectly within your rights to purchase Playboy which, we suppose, makes Sunday special in one sort of way.

215. Breeches Banished

Religious laws tend to make life a little duller, but occasionally some free-spirited local parson will pass a bylaw that makes going to church much more fun. For example, in Sheffield in 1820 this deed was drawn up: 'under no circumstances whatever shall any preacher who wears trousers be allowed to occupy the pulpit'. And in Winchester, Massachusetts, no young lady may be employed to dance on a tightrope, UNLESS she does so in church.

Old-Fashioned Justice

216. I Got it in My Change, Honest

There are some crimes that the law gets really, really uptight about. Take forgery, for instance. Obviously it's a bad thing but, in 1562, an Act in England proclaimed that the guilty party should be punished by paying twice the costs and damages of their swindle, then by being put in the pillory in the marketplace to have 'both his ears cut off, and also his nostrils be slit and cut, and seared with irons'. Then all his land was forfeit and he was jailed for life.

217. A Prisoner in His Own Home

Until Victorian times, English prisons were very different to the institutions we think of today. The places were more like walled slums than correctional facilities, and if you were rich you could buy decent food and booze, bribe the guards for better conditions and even have your family in there with you. After a Major John Bernardi went to Newgate Prison in 1689 he was forgotten about by the justice system for 47 years – at which point he died, still without having had a trial. Nevertheless, he and his wife had managed to raise 10 children in that time.

218. Ancient ASBO

According to an Act of 1405 that has never been repealed, every village in the UK with authority to govern its inhabitants must have its own set of stocks. If not, it can be officially downgraded to a hamlet. This medieval ritual of restraining unfortunate people in one location to suffer mental and physical abuse for public enjoyment might seem barbaric – until you consider *I'm A Celebrity…*

219. The Language of Litigation

You haven't been able to use a language other than English in British legal matters since 1362, when a statute forbade the use of French in court proceedings (as had been common since the Norman Conquest). Unless you're the Queen, that is. She still gives her assent to bills using Norman French: 'La Reyne le veult'. (The Queen wills it.) Mind you, given that most legal documents are written in impenetrable gibberish rather than English, we're not sure how seriously this law is taken.

220. Free to Do What You Like

Being a Freeman of London is a privilege dating back to 1237 that originally allowed craftsmen who were not the property of a feudal lord to move freely about the city. Now a civic honour, it still confers some strange rights. Freemen can drive their sheep over London Bridge, wander the city with a drawn sword, marry in St Paul's Cathedral and be drunk and disorderly without being arrested. The fact that this bonkers tradition is centred on the UK's financial and economic centre is a complete coincidence.

221. I'm Not Going South of the Tiber, Mate

The London Congestion Charge, enacted in 2003, may be one of the most ridiculous pieces of legislation – well, according to your average cabbie, that is. But it's hardly new: Julius Caesar brought in a similar statute more than 2,000 years ago banning chariots from Rome's centre to ease congestion. Chariots from the Carthaginian Embassy were probably dodging it, too.

222. Heading Back to Wales

The Welsh borderlands were a feisty place in the early 15th century. Owen Glendower led a damaging rebellion, and the Earl of Chester (later Henry V) fought back with some tough anti-Welsh legislation in 1403. He commanded all Welsh people and their sympathisers to be exiled from Chester and added: 'No Welshman may enter the city before sunrise or tarry in it after sunset on pain of decapitation'. No one is sure if this statute has been repealed, so leek-eaters on a night out – beware…

223. Battling Bureaucracy

Trial by combat was an ancient custom that allowed an accused to battle his accusers rather than go to court. Long thought extinct, it was cited in December 2002, when 60-year-old mechanic Leon Humphreys was fined £25 for failing to tell the Driver and Vehicle Licensing Agency that his Suzuki motorcycle was now off-road. He refused to pay and claimed his right to trial by combat with a 'champion' nominated by the DVLA. Killjoy magistrates in Bury St Edmunds rejected his claim and he was further fined.

224. Student Street-Walking

In 1561, Elizabeth I passed a Charter that put the city of Cambridge under the jurisdiction of its university. In 1591, Oxford University got similar powers, apparently for the 'suppressing of vice'. What this meant was that the university's constables could arrest any young ladies for the heinous crime of 'walking with a member of the university' – a polite way of saying that they were prostitutes. This legislation is still in force, so you undergrads had better think carefully about who you wander with of an evening….

225. I Swear to Eat the Truth, the Whole Truth and Nothing But the Truth

Courts in China once came up with a unique way of proving the truthfulness of suspects: they gave the accused a handful of dry rice to eat. An innocent person would simply chew and eat the grains, whereas a guilty party would have a dry mouth and so be unable to swallow. Unless of course, the rice came with some really nice stir-fried beef. Mmmm…

226. What an Ordeal

One of the grisliest ancient English laws was 'trial by ordeal', under which the accused had to carry a red-hot lump of iron down the nave of a church, or walk blindfolded over hot coals. When the mother of Edward the Confessor, Queen Emma, was accused of having it off with the Bishop of Winchester, she had to pace blindfolded over nine white-hot ploughshares. She promptly did so and insouciantly asked when the ordeal was going to start. Queens were tough in those days.

227. A Bird in the Hand

If someone owes you £1, you can't just accept 99p back, even if you really aren't bothered about the penny. The Master of the Rolls, Mr Justice Jessel, cleared this up in 1881: 'A creditor can accept anything to settle a debt, except for a lesser amount of money. He might take a horse, or a canary, or a tomtit if he chose, and that was accord and satisfaction but, by a most extraordinary peculiarity of English Common Law, he could not take 19s 6d in the pound'. Which makes it rather surprising that wallets don't have sections for tomtits.

Men Vs Women

228. This Marriage is a Joke

Divorces used to be much harder to come by. But in the US state of Delaware there was one sure-fire way to have your marriage annulled. All you had to do was prove that 'one or both parties entered into the marriage as a jest or dare'. Although the fact that someone had dared you to marry them really ought to have set alarm bells – not wedding bells – ringing.

229. This Marriage is Going Down the Toilet

Back in the days when you could only get a divorce in the UK by an Act of Parliament, one hen-pecked but very enterprising town clerk inserted the following text in clause 64 of a waterworks Bill: 'and the marriage of the Town Clerk… is hereby dissolved'. The rest of the Bill was such a turgid tome of sewer-speak and water-waffle that no one noticed and the Bill was enacted. The town clerk was then legally divorced.

230. Run for Your Wives

Women may have the vote in most countries, but the law still discriminates against them in many ways. In Vermont, for example, women must obtain written permission from their husbands to wear false teeth. While a Michigan state law decrees that a wife's hair legally belongs to her husband. And when women drive in Memphis, 'a man must walk or run in front of the vehicle, waving a red flag in order to warn approaching pedestrians and motorists'. Seems like a good way to keep your fella on his toes...

231. Sexist Statutes... 1

In Montana, it is a felony for a wife to open her husband's mail. Kentucky wives need spousal permission to buy hats, and Ohio women are forbidden from wearing patent leather shoes, in case men see the reflection of their underwear. (Society would obviously break down if that happened.)

232. Sexist Statutes... 2

The boys don't have it all their own way. In Cold Spring, Pennsylvania, wives must give written permission if a married man wants to buy alcohol. Meanwhile, girls in Kentucky are legally allowed to slip castor oil into their husbands' drinks to stop them imbibing too much booze. Although that could seriously, ahem, backfire on them in the middle of the night.

233. One for the Boys

Gentlemen, if your lovely lady is badgering you to accompany her on a shopping trip, you might want to think about taking her to Joliet, Illinois. If she tries on more than six dresses in one shop, she will be arrested, and you can spend your afternoon more usefully. Just remember to practise saying the town name before you go, though; in Joliet it is illegal to mispronounce 'Joliet'.

234. Clean out of Coffee

You might think that California would have Saudi Arabia beat real good when it comes to women's legal rights. But that state still insists that housewives must boil their dusters after use, at the risk of a fine or jail sentence. Whereas Saudi Arabian wives can divorce their husbands straight off the bat if they don't provide them with regular amounts of coffee.

235. Slanderous Southerners

Gossip columnists beware – it is still illegal under the Slander of Women Act 1891 to 'impute unchastity or adultery' to a woman in England, Wales or Ireland. If you're in Scotland, however, you can call every lass you meet a tart or a strumpet, and the law can't touch you – but their 6-foot tall, porridge-eating, caber-tossing boyfriends just might, though…

236. Mucking Out

Wives in Hereford have one very important matrimonial right enshrined in law – that of being allowed to throw out their husband's nudie magazines, blue movies and other sexual materials that he may have stashed behind the flowerpots in his shed. Reports that this law has been updated to include the bookmarks in his web browser have not been verified.

237. Women's Wiles

But it's Nottingham's single men who are protected by ancient statute. There, no woman may 'fraudulently and deceitfully' entice a bachelor away from his mother to trap him in a 'clandestine marriage'. The Nottingham judiciary is still deciding on whether fake tan, hair extensions and Wonderbras count as fraud and deceit.

238. Matrimonial Mentalists

Ministers in Pennsylvania are forbidden from performing marriages when either the bride or groom is drunk. And it's illegal to discharge a gun, revolver or indeed a cannon at a wedding, no matter how exciting things get. In Rhode Island, any marriage in which either of the parties turns out to be a lunatic or an idiot is declared null and void. Depending on your definition of 'idiot' that could open the door to a LOT of divorces.

Daft
Defences

239. Murder in the Matrix

In July 2002, Tonda Lynn Ansley of Ohio shot her landlady in the head. At her trial for murder, Ansley's attorneys argued that she believed that 'our world is just an illusion generated by our machine overlords' similar to those in the film *The Matrix*. They claimed that Ansley thought she was inside a computer simulation and her landlady was part of a plan to 'brainwash and murder' her. The jury found her not guilty by reason of insanity, before Keanu could kick down the doors and rescue her.

240. A Twinkie in His Eye

In 1978, Dan White assassinated San Francisco City Supervisor Harvey Milk and Mayor George Moscone. A psychiatrist called by the defence testified that White had been severely depressed at the time of the crime, as was shown by the fact that he had given up his usually very healthy diet and started scoffing high-sugar junk foods and fizzy drinks. A journalist coined this the 'Twinkie Defence'. Jurors swallowed it and convicted him of voluntary manslaughter rather than murder.

241. I Didn't Like the Way He Looked at Me

When Joseph Biedermann was accused of first-degree murder in 2009, he claimed he had committed the crime while in a 'gay panic'. Biedermann said that his neighbour, Terrance Hauser, made unwanted sexual advances on him after a drinking session and he then lashed out with a knife 'in self defence'. Despite the fact that Biedermann had 'defended himself' by inflicting 61 separate stab wounds, the jury in Cook County, Illinois, found him not guilty. Something tells us this defence is going to get used again…

242. He Promised Me a Special Bonus

Anne Frank of Connecticut filed a lawsuit against the city of Greenwich, where she worked as a clerk in the parks and recreation department, claiming $25,000 in unpaid wages. This was for extra work she had to take on while her boss was having an affair with his secretary. Frank alleges he said she could claim the hours back, but the department director refused to pay the extra salary. What do office trysts go on the timesheet as?

243. I'll Get My Brother On You

When Sathis Raj was arrested in Malaysia with 166 kilos of cannabis and 1.7 kilos of raw opium in 2003, things looked bad – like death-by-hanging bad. The prosecution probably broke out the Champagne – they had Raj red-handed at the scene and his DNA on the stash. The only problem was that Sathis had an identical twin, Sabarish Raj, and each claimed the other did it. They looked so alike that judge and jury couldn't be sure which twin was arrested at the scene of the crime, and identical twins have identical DNA. The men walked free.

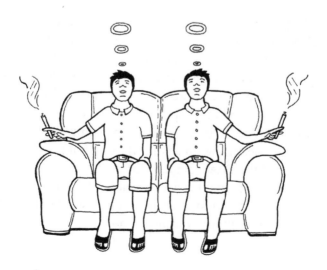

244. Busted

When a Japanese girl was accused of breaking into her boyfriend's apartment, her lawyers came up with a very creative defence. They claimed that it couldn't have been her who crawled through the hole in the door made by the burglar because… her breasts were too large. It was perfectly apparent to everyone in the court that they had made two very fine points. The girl was freed and her supporters were delighted.

245. Reasonable Doubt

Marcy Noriega, a California police officer, had just bundled a suspect into the back of her cop car in Madera City when he became violent. Noriega instantly drew her Taser and used it to calm the man – except it wasn't her Taser that she had drawn but her gun, and the suspect was calm because he was stone dead. Obviously the man's family filed a wrongful death lawsuit against the city, but the city then sued the Taser company for the full costs of the death suit, arguing that a 'reasonable' officer could mistakenly draw and shoot their gun instead of their Taser. Sounds pretty reasonable, no?

And Finally...

Lawyers Being the Ass

246. The Killing Joke

A Representative of the Texas Legislature, Tom Moore Jr, was so sick of the Law's ass-like behaviour in his state that he introduced a very special Resolution. It ostensibly honoured one Albert de Salvo for his 'unconventional techniques involving population control' and was duly passed in 1971. Moore then pointed out that de Salvo was the 'Boston Strangler', murderer of 13 women in the 1960s.
His point that legislators pass bills without actually reading them was considered proven.

247. The $65 Million Pants

R oy Pearson from Washington DC wanted to wear his favourite suit on his first day in a new job, but a dry cleaner lost the trousers. Pearson decided this had ruined his life, so he sued the family business for $65,462,500 – an amount calculated to cover his 'mental suffering, inconvenience and discomfort', and 10 years' worth of weekend car rentals so he can transport his dry cleaning to another store. The Superior Court judge wasn't moved – he castigated Pearson for his 'bad faith' and awarded damages to the dry cleaners. And Pearson really should have known better – his new job was as an Administrative Law Judge.

248. Playing the Legal Game

When a hotel investment firm sued an insurance company for allegedly not paying an insurance claim fast enough after Hurricane Charley, the particularly bellicose attorneys could not agree on even where a witness would be deposed. US District Judge Gregory Presnell was not amused at their shenanigans and issued this written ruling: '… at 4pm on Friday, June 30, 2006, counsel shall convene at a neutral site agreeable to both parties… At that time and location, counsel shall engage in one (1) game of 'rock, paper, scissors'. The winner of this engagement shall be entitled to select the location for the 30(b)(6) deposition.'

249. Goods as Described

An attorney in Southern California filed a lawsuit against phone company GTE for being listed in their Yellow Pages under the heading 'Reptiles'. The attorney alleged he became the target of jokes, rude telephone calls, hissing noises and other forms of ridicule, and claimed damages in excess of $100,000. The error was due to the attorney's telephone number being reassigned from a defunct business named the 'Reptile Show', and GTE not updating its records. He should, of course, correctly have been listed under 'Sharks'.

250. Double Trouble

A Los Angeles lawyer representing himself in a case for recovery of his fees had his claim dismissed because he failed to appear for a scheduled court hearing. Showing considerable front, he later filed a motion requesting relief from this dismissal based upon the theory that it wouldn't be fair to penalise the client for the mistakes of his lawyer. Or, presumably, from hiring such an idiot in the first place.

The End

Acknowledgements

I'd especially like to thank Gareth Tenner for some juicy examples and JP Campbell of The Elephant Juice Soup Company for some fine legal tales and some equally inspiring soup.

Bibliography – the titles I have principally used as reference are *The Strange Laws of Old England* by Nigel Cawthorne (Piatkus, 2004) and *Odd Laws* by Jenny Paschall & Ron Lyon (HarperCollins, 1996). I have also used the following websites to research this book: blogs.loc.gov, dumblaws.com, en.wikipedia.org, idiotlaws.com, itthing.com, kristleywd3.hubpages.com, lawguru.com, lawcommission.justice.gov.uk, peoriamagazines.com, strangefacts.com, turtlezen.com.

The Law Is An Ass
Concept: Amy Sheldrake
Researched and written by: Richard Happer
Illustrations: Joseph Hemmings (*www.josephhemmings.com*)

Managing Editor: Sophie Dawson
Design & Cover: Harriet Yeomans
Proofreader: Leanne Bryan
Marketing: Shelley Bowdler
Publisher: Jonathan Knight

Published by:
Punk Publishing,
3 The Yard, Pegasus Place,
London
SE11 5SD